The Greek revival   J. Mordaunt Crook

Both the Greek and Gothic revivals in Brit
earnest almost simultaneously. Sanderson Miller's Gothic ruin at
Hagley Park in Worcestershire dates from 1747. James Stuart's Doric
temple in the same park dates from 1758. Both buildings were products
of Romanticism, just as much as Sir William Chambers' Chinese
pagoda in Kew Gardens. But the progress of these parallel movements
was very different. The Greek revival became respectable and scholarly
two generations sooner than the Gothic. By the 1840s when the Gothic
revival was beginning to move into its dominant, High Church phase,
the Greek revival was almost over – in England, if not in Scotland.
These contrasting rates of progress can be explained very largely in
terms of archaeological publications: it was not until the 1830s that
Gothic revival architects had at their fingertips a range of stylistic
precedents comparable to the volumes of Greek antiquities published
during the second half of the 18th century. When the Gothic revival
was eventually regularized by a group of Cambridge High Churchmen
known as the Ecclesiological or Camden Society, an organisational
precedent already existed. For during the previous three quarters of
a century a group of rich patrons known as the Society of Dilettanti
had regularized the Greek revival by systematically encouraging
archaeological accuracy. If there is a parallel between the two
movements, there is also a striking chronological difference.

The basis of Greek revivalism was an upsurge of interest in Grecian
antiquities. During the second half of the 18th century, the ancient
sites in Italy, Sicily and Asia Minor – Paestum, Palmyra, Baalbek and
Spalato (Split) had been drawn into the circuit of the Grand Tour and
had supplied an archaeological framework for the so-called 'Etruscan'
styles of Robert Adam in architecture and interior decoration and
Josiah Wedgwood in pottery. During the Napoleonic Wars, which
closed most of Europe to British travellers, Greece, as part of the

Plate 1
James Elmes (1782–1862)
Basilica and temples of Poseidon
and Demeter at Paestum
Watercolour 18¾ × 27in.
Presented by H. S. Goodhart-Rendel, 1940
The father of the architect H. L. Elmes
(see plates 35–40), James Elmes was an
architectural writer best known as editor of
Shepherd's *Metropolitan Improvements* (1829)
and author of the first documented
life of Wren.

neutral Turkish Empire, still remained open to the Grand Tourist.
The British navy dominated the Mediterranean and Nelson became
a popular hero among the Greeks. A wave of romantic hellenism
reinvigorated the old humanistic tradition. The early Georgian
cosmopolite emerged as the sentimental traveller of the Regency:
Lord Byron succeeded Lord Burlington. Some of the early pioneers
in Greece were Frenchmen like J. D. Le Roy, but most of them were
English: Stuart and Revett, Dawkins and Wood, Chandler, Thomas
Hope, Moritt and Tweddell. From 1801 onwards there appeared a
veritable flood of British travellers. In the first five years of the century
these included the Elgin contingent, the man Byron christened 'rapid'
Gell, the architects Robert Smirke and William Wilkins, and
'Athenian' Aberdeen, the future Prime Minister. They were followed
by a number of budding architects during the next decade, including
J. P. Gandy, Francis Bedford, C. R. Cockerell and W. H. Inwood –
all of whom published their discoveries. This phase of archaeological
investigation is nicely illustrated by five drawings from the RIBA
collection: the picturesque view of the Erechtheum at Athens from
Stuart and Revett's *Antiquities of Athens* (plate 5); James Elmes's
dramatic view of Paestum (plate 1); two sketches of the ruins at
Bassae and Agrigentum by Robert Smirke and C. R. Cockerell
(plates 2, 3); and Francis Bedford's reconstruction of the temple at
Eleusis (plate 4).

Half a century of travel and tourism culminated in the Regency
period – roughly speaking, the first three decades of the 19th century.
The result was a mass of archaeological publications, replete with
measured drawings, plans, cross-sections and elevations of the principal
Greek antiquities. The most influential books were: Richard Dalton's
Museum Graecum et Aegypticum (1751), Le Roy's *Ruines des Plus Beaux
Monuments de la Grèce* (1758), Robert Sayer's *Ruins of Athens and
Other Valuable Antiquities in Greece* (1759), Winckelmann's
Observations on the Architecture of the Ancients (1762) and *History*

Plate 2
Sir Robert Smirke (1780–1867)
Temple of Apollo at Bassae
Watercolour 20¼ × 28in.
Presented by Smirke's son-in-law
Captain G. R. Lambert, 1895
Smirke travelled abroad between 1801 and
1805. The RIBA possesses a remarkable
collection of his letters, journals, sketches
and plans. Together they add up to a
day-by-day account of the making of a
Greek revivalist.

Plate 3
Charles Robert Cockerell (1788–1863)
Temple of Hera Lacinia at Agrigentum
from the south west in 1812

Pen and wash 15⅞ × 10½in.
Presented by Mrs F. M. Noel
Literature:
J. Addison, RIBA Journal, XXXIX, 1932,
p.165; A. T. Bolton, RIBA Journal, XL, 1933,
p.798
The prince of British classicists, Cockerell
first made his name as an archaeologist.
He travelled abroad between 1810–17,
making a number of celebrated discoveries,
including the Aegina and Phigaleian marbles.
Sir Charles Eastlake, the painter, wrote
in 1817: 'Of all the artists who are [in Rome]
...Cockerell...is one of the cleverest...
He has brought a most valuable portfolio of
drawings from Greece. I heard of him
as soon as I arrived.'

of Ancient Art (1764), Dumont's *Ruins of Paestum* (1764), T. Major's
Ruines de Paestum, ou de Poséidonie dans la Grande Grèce (1768),
S. Riou's *Grecian Orders of Architecture Delineated and Explained*
(1768), Revett's *Ionian Antiquities* (1769 and 1797), Gandy and
Bedford's *Unedited Antiquities of Attica* (1817), William Wilkins's
Magna Graecia (1807), W. H. Inwood's *Fragments of Athenian
Architecture* (1827) and, of course, Stuart and Revett's seminal
Antiquities of Athens in three fine folios 1762, 1787 and 1794, plus two
posthumous volumes largely edited by C. R. Cockerell in 1816 and
1830. James Stuart and Nicholas Revett were the twin arbiters of the
new fashion. Sir John Soane christened them 'the classical Stuart
and the indefatigable Revett'. Certainly their publications simplified
the whole process of design. Compare James Wyatt's pigeon house
at Badger (plate 8) with Stuart and Revett's illustration of the Tower
of the Winds (plate 6) or J. M. Gandy's romantic temple (plate 9) with
their corresponding illustration of the Choragic Monument of
Lysicrates (plate 7). Decimus Burton was thus able to make his name
as a Greek revivalist (plate 31) before he had time to visit Greece.

So much for archaeology's part in the Greek revival. What of the
theory behind it, the philosophy of revivalism? The Greek revival
was an international movement in its own right, the last chapter in the
story of European classicism, the culmination of the Neo-classical
phase in western art. But it was also one aspect of an even wider
movement, namely romanticism. Romanticism was a rebellion against
the formality and restraint of classical tradition in literature and the
arts in general. In relation to architecture, this rebellion meant a new
wave of eclecticism, historicism and experimentalism – that is, the
selection of historical styles and motifs according to archaeological
precedent, and their combination in accordance with new theories
of composition. To describe the architecture of romanticism,
historians generally use two alternative labels: Romantic Classicism
or Neo-classicism. Both of these neologisms signify an attitude rather

Plate 4

Francis Octavius Bedford (1784–1858)
Reconstructed interior of the Propylaea at
Eleusis, showing Doric and Ionic columns
Pen with touches of wash 9½ × 13in.
Presented by the Society of Dilettanti, 1912
Bedford visited Greece and Asia Minor in
1811–13 in company with
J. P. Gandy-Deering, Sir William Gell
and J. Walker on an expedition sponsored
by the Society of Dilettanti. The results
of their researches, including an engraving
of this drawing, were published in 1817
as *Unedited Antiquities of Attica*.

than a style, a revolution in composition, not just a novel system of decoration. Neo-classicism transcended such purely stylistic categories as the 'Grecian', 'Italian', 'Gothic' and 'Egyptian'. It was self-consciously anti-Baroque and similarly anti-Palladian. Baroque architects had aimed at plasticity in design and comprehension in plan. They made use of classical elements decoratively rather than· functionally. Neo-classical architects repudiated these Renaissance assumptions. They aimed at rigidity in design and disparity in plan. They demanded the truthful use of classical orders – their columns at least *appeared* to support something. Above all, instead of taking classical architecture at second or third hand, via Vitruvius or Palladio, they became archaeologists and went back to the original evidence. Neo-classical architecture traced its ancestry from several Continental sources: from the visionary drawings of the Italian Piranesi and the German Friedrick Gilly; from the rationalist theories of three great architectural philosophers, Cordemoy, Laugier and Blondel; and from the ruthlessly geometric designs of architects like Boullée and Ledoux, who prospered during the period of the French revolution. Neo-classicism grew to maturity during the second half of the 18th century, consolidated by educators like Durand in France, Valadier in Italy and Soane and Dance in England. The style's universal validity at the dawn of the 19th century recalls the dominance of the modernist school in intellectual circles during the early decades of the 20th century.

In Britain, these ideas mingled with our home-grown philosophy of the Picturesque: the principles of landscape composition developed during the 18th century by William Kent, 'Capability' Brown, Humphry Repton, Payne Knight and Uvedale Price – a system of visual values fusing architecture with nature in a series of scenic entities. British Greek revival architecture was therefore the product of two forces: Neo-classicism and the Picturesque. The essence of Neo-classical architecture lay in its synthesis of archaeological detail and

Plate 5
James Stuart (1713–88)
View of the Erechtheum on the Acropolis
at Athens from the west, showing the
Caryatid porch and the artist sketching.
Gouache 10¾ × 15⅛in.
Presented by the Executors of
Thomas Howard, 1873
Literature:
Lesley Lawrence, Journal of the Warburg
Institute, II, 1938–9

Antiquities of Athens, in which this was
engraved as pl. ii of Vol. II, Chapter II,
made 'Athenian' Stuart something of an
arbiter of taste. His natural indolence,
however, made his influence posthumous
rather than contemporary. A detail of this
picture appears in colour on the cover.

9

Plates 6, 7
James Stuart and **Nicholas Revett**
(1720–1804)
Engravings from *Antiquities of Athens* I
(1762), ch. III, pl. iii and ch. IV, pl. iii
left
The Tower of the Winds at Athens
right
The Choragic Monument of Lysicrates at
Athens (built to commemorate the success
of a chorus in the theatre, but known
colloquially during the 18th century as
'Demosthenes' Lanthorn').
Literature:
Hugh Honour, Country Life, CXXIII,
1958, pp.1120, 1379; Christopher Hussey,
Country Life, CXV, 1954, pp.1126–9, 1220–3
Both buildings were widely copied by
Greek revivalists. The Tower of the Winds
appears *inter alia* at the Radcliffe Observatory
in Oxford, St Pancras New Church in London
(plate 21) and at Badger Hall, Shropshire
(plate 8). The Lysicrates monument made an
ideal model for garden temples and funeral
monuments up and down the country.

Plate 8
James Wyatt (1746–1813)
Pigeon house (columbarium) at
Badger Hall, Shropshire, 1780
Pen 22¾ × 14in.
Badger Hall was built to Wyatt's designs

for Isaac Hawkins Browne in 1779–83,
and was demolished in 1952, though its
classical garden temple survives.
The pigeon house is taken directly from
Stuart and Revett's engraving of the
Tower of the Winds (plate 6).

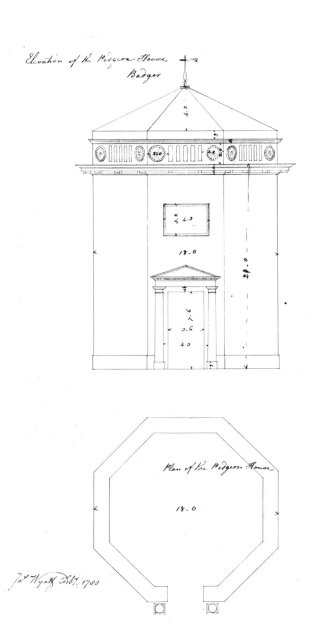

geometrical forms. The essence of Picturesque composition, as applied to architecture, was its emphasis on variety, irregularity and contrast. To a greater or lesser degree, all Greek revival architecture reflects the influence of these ideas.

It was only after 1800 that the Grecian style really got a grip on Britain. Regency architects adopted it with greater speed and accuracy than they did the Gothic – with greater speed because of the strength of the hellenist fashion and with greater accuracy both because of the archaeological publications already mentioned and because Regency architects were natural classicists, working within the Georgian tradition. During the 1820s, the Grecian style was supreme throughout the western world. These were the years of the Greek War of Independence (1821–33), the poetry of Byron, Keats, Shelley and Landor, the sculpture of Flaxman, Thorwaldsen, Westmacott and Chantrey and the architecture of Schinkel in Germany, of William Strickland in the United States, of Robert Smirke and William Wilkins in England and of Thomas Hamilton and W. H. Playfair in Scotland. Thereafter there was a swift decline in England but not in Scotland.

In the forty years before it caught on, the Greek revival had been developing outside the mainstream of British architecture. In this period of the movement's genesis, between 1753 and 1800, the key names are James Stuart, Nicholas Revett, Benjamin Latrobe, Joseph Bonomi and Thomas Harrison. Soane and Wyatt also had a considerable part to play. For example: Wyatt's work at Gresford Lodge, Cheshire (c 1790) and Ottershaw Park, Surrey (c 1795); Soane's work at Hammels Park, Hertfordshire (1783), Langley Park, Norfolk (1786), Sydney Lodge, Hampshire (1789), Tyringham, Buckinghamshire (1792–5) and Bentley Priory near Stanmore (1798). But it is the names of Stuart, Revett, Latrobe, Bonomi and Harrison which are persistently associated with the earliest use of the Doric order, fluted or unfluted. The history of the movement revolves round a few celebrated items: Stuart's temples at Hagley and Shugborough (1758);

Plate 9
Joseph Michael Gandy (1771–1843)
Design for a monument
Signed on base of monument
ΓΑΝΔI αρχιτεχτω (Gandy built this)
Pen and watercolour,
with ruled and wash border 18¾ × 14¾in.
Presented by Richard Westmacott, 1862
Literature:
Sir J. Summerson *Heavenly Mansions*
(1949), ch. V

Gandy's source for this design, with a stone
pyre set on a rock overlooking the sea and a
small tetrastyle Ionic temple behind it,
was, of course, the Choragic Monument of
Lysicrates (plate 7). He was much
employed as a draughtsman by
Sir John Soane. Gandy's visionary
schemes have earned him the title of
the 'English Piranesi'.

Revett's use at Standlynch, Wiltshire (*c* 1766) and Ayot St. Lawrence, Buckinghamshire (1778) of the semi-fluted Doric order from the Temple of Apollo at Delos; Latrobe's work at Hammerwood and Ashdown in Sussex (1793–4); Bonomi's remarkable church at Great Packington, Warwickshire (1789); and Harrison's monumental Chester Castle (1785–1820), with which the Greek revival comes of age. Benjamin H. Latrobe, of course, is a figure of international rather than national significance. He emigrated to Virginia in 1796 and lived to transform American architecture. In Sir John Summerson's words, at the Bank of Philadelphia in 1798 he 'married English Neo-classicism to Jeffersonian Neo-classicism [and] . . . from that moment, the classical revival in America took on a national form'.

The failure of the Grecian style to establish itself in Britain before about 1800 can be attributed to several causes. Firstly there was Revett's lack of ambition and Stuart's unbusinesslike manner (even his masterpiece, the chapel at Greenwich (plate 10), was re-designed and largely executed by his assistant, William Newton). Then there was the fact of Thomas Harrison's geographical isolation. His remarkable designs (plates 15, 16, 17) had little influence in London. As one partisan provincial critic put it in 1843, it was to be 'regretted that Harrison had buried his fine talents in the little obscure city of Chester, instead of settling in London and correcting the bad taste of Nash, Soane and others'. Most of all, however, there was the bitter opposition of professional antagonists, the 'anti-Greeks': Sir William Chambers, learned in Renaissance tradition and backed up by a fellow-Palladian, James Paine; and Robert Adam, anxious to popularize his own 'Etruscan' style. Writing in 1823, James Elmes remembered how most architects had hated 'the new-fangled "Doric" without a base, as much as they did a shirt without ruffles, or a wig without two good portly curls over each ear, and half a yard of tail behind; scorning its simpler flutes without fillets, which they compared to ribbed stockings'. Instead, they admired 'the rusticated and twisted columns of Batty

Plate 10
James Stuart
Chapel of the Royal Hospital, Greenwich
Design for interior decoration of the west
end after the fire, 1782
Pen and wash 16 × 24in. (fly-leaf, 13¼ × 4¾in.)
Presented by the Governors of the
Royal Naval Academy
Literature:
Lesley Lewis, Art Bulletin, XXXIX, 1947
'Athenian' Stuart was Surveyor of
Greenwich Hospital from 1758 until his
death thirty years later. In this capacity he
was responsible for the exquisite Grecian
decoration of the reconstructed chapel,
1779–88. This drawing is inscribed
*The capitals and bases of the columns, and the
principal door case, to be of white marble, the
columns to be of Scagliola in imitation of
Giallo antico.* Much of the work was,
however, left to his assistant, William Newton,
who probably increased the archaeological
content of the original designs. By later
revivalist standards, Stuart's work was
insufficiently 'chaste'.

Langley . . . [they] lamented the shocking innovations of Wyatt and Soane, the more dreadful importations of Stuart, and were nearly going into a fever when the portico at Covent Garden Theatre was opened'. Adam described Stuart's work at Spencer House in London as 'pitifulissimo'; the ceilings might be 'Greek to the teeth . . . but by God they are not handsome'.

So a distinction is easily drawn between the development of the Grecian style in England between the 1760s and the 1790s and its propagation during the Regency period. The six years 1803–9 were crucial. Before 1803, the Greek revival had developed as one of several exotic styles produced by the romantic impulse. After 1810 it was not only fashionable, it was the very criterion of architectural distinction. In 1803–6, George Dance reconstructed Stratton Park, Hampshire, using a Paestum-proportioned unfluted Doric portico and a staircase with primitive Doric columns borrowed from Dubut's *Maisons de Ville et de Campagne* (1803). Dance's legacy to Regency classicism, *via* two of his pupils, was twofold: firstly the elision or paring down of classical elements demonstrated at All Hallows and the London Guildhall Council Chamber and continued by Soane; and secondly the combination of Greek orders and cubic severity demonstrated at Stratton and continued by Smirke.

In 1804, Wilkins defeated Wyatt in the competition for Downing College, Cambridge, with the help of a fighting pamphlet by a rich and influential connoisseur, Thomas Hope. In 1805, Wilkins defeated Henry Holland in a parallel competition for the East India College at Haileybury. Both competitions were cases of the Greek Ionic defeating the Roman Doric (plates 13, 14). In 1806, Dance produced an Ionic portico in London at the Royal College of Surgeons, Lincoln's Inn Fields. In 1809, Wilkin's Doric portico at Grange Park (plate 23) put nearby Stratton in the shade, and Smirke's Doric Covent Garden became the talk of the capital. From then onwards the fashion swept the country. Within twelve months, William Stokoe had carried

Plate 11 (*above*)
Attributed to **William Wilkins** (1778–1839)
Unexecuted design for a college in
Regent's Park, London, *c* 1828
Watercolour 9¼ × 19¼in.
Presented by John Harris, 1961
University College, London, was begun in
1827 to the designs of Wilkins and
J. P. Gandy-Deering. Two years later,
King's College, London, an Anglican and
Tory foundation, was set up as a
counter-attraction to the Benthamism
of Gower Street. Before Smirke's building
in the Strand was begun, several alternative
sites were discussed. One of these was the
Inner Circle in Nash's newly created
Regent's Park. Neighbouring residents
successfully protested that 'one Zoo
was enough'.

Plate 12 (*right*)
William Wilkins
Design for a Doric lodge at
Stourhead, Wiltshire
Perspective of a proposed obelisk and
other buildings in the landscape for
Sir R. Colt Hoare, 1815
Pen and watercolour 22½ × 35½in.
Exhibited at the Royal Academy, 1817
The Stourhead landscape as a whole is the
locus classicus of 'the Picturesque'.
This particular design was never executed,
but there is a letter at Stourhead from Wilkins,
dated 1815, claiming payment of £60 18*s.*
for making it.

Plate 13
William Wilkins
Downing College, Cambridge
Perspective (perhaps by J. Bailey) of the
successful design, showing the
unexecuted central block.
Watercolour $11\frac{1}{2} \times 21\frac{1}{2}$in.
Presented by M. A. Harry Heron
Literature:
G. Walkley, RIBA Journal, XLV, 1938, p.1014;
J. M. Crook *Haileybury and the Greek Revival:
the Architecture of William Wilkins, RA.* (1964)

In 1804, Wilkins defeated James Wyatt in
the competition for the college. It was
something of a *cause célèbre* in the story of
the Greek revival. Lewis Wyatt and
George Byfield were also-rans. Wilkins's
success meant not only the triumph of Greek
over Roman orders but the victory of
campus over quadrangle, for Downing was
the first college with a campus-style layout
of contiguous blocks, ten years earlier
than Jefferson's University of Virginia.

Plate 14
James Wyatt Downing
Defeated competition design for College,
first submitted in 1784
Perspective of the proposed quadrangle
Pen and watercolour within framed black
ruled border 12½ × 31 in.
Wyatt's quadrangular design in the
Roman Doric style was defeated by
Wilkins's Greek revival scheme,
seen in plate 13.

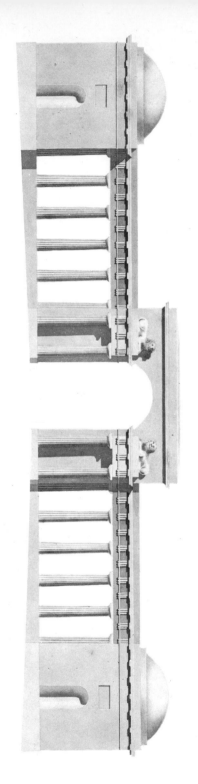

Smirke's Covent Garden as far North as Newcastle-upon-Tyne in the shape of his sturdy Doric Moot Hall. In buildings as different as Barry's Manchester Institution, now the City Art Gallery (1823), Inwood's St. Pancras Church, London (1819–22, plate 21) and Smirke's British Museum (1823–51, plates 25, 26), the Greek revival reached its culmination in England. The work of prolific provincial architects like Haycock of Shrewsbury, Foulston of Plymouth, Foster of Liverpool and Lane and Goodwin of Manchester ensured the spread of the new style throughout the country during the 1820s and 1830s.

Wales and Ireland have their share of Greek revival monuments. For example, Brecon Shire Hall (T. H. Wyatt, 1842) and the Roman Catholic Pro-Cathedral at Dublin (John Sweetman, 1816–25). But neither country produced a native Greek revival tradition. Things were very different in Scotland. Here the dissemination of the style was less rapid than in England but much more complete. Perhaps grey stone Grecian buildings suited the chilly northern temperament. Perhaps the Grecian style expressed religious hostility to the liturgical enthusiasm of High Anglican Gothic. Either way, north of the border the fashion enjoyed an Indian Summer which lasted even beyond the high Victorian period. The movement begins with the Glasgow Courthouse (c 1807–14) by the shadowy William Stark. This building boasted a Doric portico which certainly rivalled and probably antedated Smirke's Covent Garden. During the next few decades, David Hamilton and Archibald Simpson fully maintained the Glaswegian tradition of Greek revivalism, but the biggest opportunities occurred in the New Town at Edinburgh. For this was the 'Athens of the North'. Archibald Elliot set the pace with his use of the Ionic order at Waterloo Place (1815–19) and County Hall (1816–19). William Burn proved himself an apt pupil of Smirke with his Doric New Academy (1822–4) and John Watson's School (1825) and Hospital (1835). Thereafter the stage is dominated by two architects, Thomas Hamilton and W. H. Playfair. Hamilton's Royal High School (1826–9), Playfair's Scottish Academy

Plates 15, 16, 17

Thomas Harrison (1744–1829)

Recently discovered at Chester, these three drawings show Harrison combining archaeological accuracy with compositional freedom. 15 is a variant for the entrance to Chester Castle, planned in 1784 but not finished until 1820. It is related to a number of his designs for private entrance lodges. 17 is one of several schemes by Harrison for a monumental rotunda, very much in the French *grand prix* tradition. With 16, it is probably a visionary scheme to commemorate British victories in the Napoleonic wars. Of the two, 16 can be dated more precisely: like other architects, Harrison was anxious to redevelop the Waterloo bridge area as a monumental precinct and in 1814 he exhibited at the Royal Academy 'A National Building to record by painting and sculpture the Victories of the Marquis of Wellington and other commanders by sea and land during the present war'. Perhaps this dramatic drawing shows his exhibition design framed by an arch of Rennie's Waterloo bridge.

Plate 15 (page 22)
Design for a gateway
Pen and grey wash 16 × 21 in.

Plate 16 (*below*)
Design for a military and
naval monument, 1814
Pen and grey wash 10¾ × 25 in.

Plate 17
Thomas Harrison
Design for a rotunda
Pen and coloured wash $18\frac{1}{4} \times 25$in.
(See page 24)

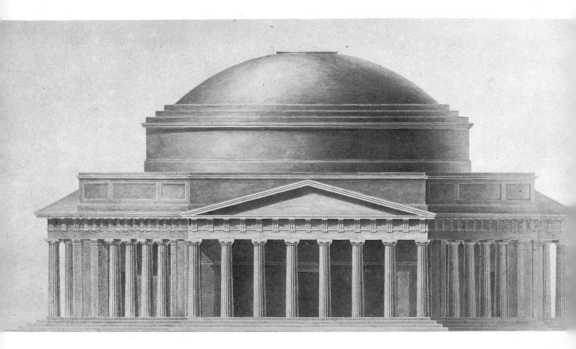

(1822–6 and 1832–5) and National Gallery (1850–7), and Cockerell and Playfair's unfinished National Monument (1822–30), as well as half a dozen conspicuous funeral trophies, brilliantly turned Calton Hill and its environs into a Caledonian Acropolis (plates 29, 30). After the middle of the century, the scene switches back to Glasgow, to the work of Alexander 'Greek' Thomson. In a remarkable series of churches, commercial buildings and residential terraces built between the 1850s and the 1870s, Thomson realised to the full the rich potentialities of the Grecian idiom.

These potentialities were compositional rather than decorative. About 1815, Smirke began a treatise on the theory and practice of architecture. It was never published, but its survival in manuscript form in the RIBA library serves as a salutary reminder that Greek revivalism was more than archaeological mimicry. The treatise forms part of the French rationalist tradition of Cordemoy, Laugier and Blondel, that is, the Neo-classical philosophy which the author imbibed from his tutors, Sir John Soane and George Dance II. According to this tradition, archaeological accuracy was subordinated to a romantic theory of functionalism, and the use of classical orders was strictly regulated by Laugier's doctrine of 'apparent utility'. Greek architecture, Smirke maintained, had degenerated in the hands of the Romans, until 'its despicable remains were almost everywhere superseded by that singular and mysterious compound of styles' known as Gothic. Renaissance architecture revived Roman forms but combined them with medieval anachronisms, 'and hence were derived the steeples, towers, pinnacles, balconies and balustrades' of Renaissance design. Even Inigo Jones and Christopher Wren had drunk of this polluted stream, while Vanbrugh, although 'his genius . . . was powerful and impressive', took over the Renaissance style, 'helped himself liberally to its vices, contributed many of his own, and by an unfortunate misfortune, adding impurity to that which was already greatly impure, left it disgusting and often odious'.

Plate 18 (*left*)
Sir Robert Smirke
Design for Whittinghame House,
East Lothian, 1817
Perspective of the entrance front
Dated *Albany, Decr. 4th 1817*
Watercolour 10 × 14½in.
Presented by H. L. Anderson, 1933
Like Kinnmount, Dumfriesshire and
Normanby Park, Lincolnshire, this is an
example of Smirke's 'Greco-cubic' style.
It was built in 1818 for James Balfour,
the son of an Indian nabob, who 'spent and
circulated in one year more money . . . than
many do in ten'. Internal alterations were
made in the 1890s by Lawrence Turner
and Eustace Balfour, brother of
the prime minister.

Plate 19 (*below*)
Design for a large country house by an
unidentified early 19th-century
English architect.
Watercolour, mounted on canvas 20 × 29½in.

Plate 20
Francis Bedford (1784–1858)
Defeated competition design for
St Pancras Church, London, 1818
Copy made in 1839 by J. Drayton Wyatt
(1820–91)
Watercolour $6\frac{1}{2} \times 4\frac{1}{2}$in.
Presented by J. D. Wyatt, 1889
Bedford was awarded the second prize
of £50, Rickman coming third. Although
defeated at St Pancras, he designed four
churches in Grecian style in London:
St George, Camberwell; St Luke,
West Norwood; Holy Trinity, Southwark;
St John, Waterloo Road. This elevation and
the winning design opposite are reproduced
in scale with each other. Bedford's tower
was to be 132 feet high and the Inwoods'
156 feet.

Plate 21
William (*c* 1771–1843) and
Henry William Inwood (1794–1843)
Church of St Pancras, London
Copy by J. D. Wyatt of the original contract
drawings as executed, 1819
West elevation.
Pen and wash 25¾ × 18in.
Presented by J. D. Wyatt, 1889

Drawing for inspiration on the Erechtheum,
the Tower of the Winds and the Lysicrates
monument, St Pancras New Church
(1819–22) was a landmark of the Greek
revival. Costing more than £70,000, it
justifies Summerson's description as
'the queen of 19th-century churches'. These
copies were made by J. D. Wyatt while
articled to H. W. Inwood, 1839–40.

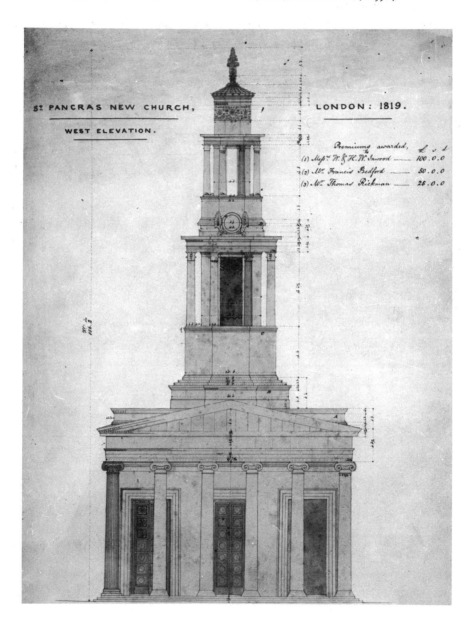

31

Plate 22
Henry Edmund Goodridge (*c* 1800–63)
Lansdown Tower, Bath, Somerset
Design made for William Beckford, 1825–6
Pen with grey and blue washes 18¼ × 11¾in.
Presented by H. E. Goodridge, 1836
William Beckford, the eccentric millionaire,
sold his 'Gothick' Fonthill Abbey
and moved to Bath in 1822. There he
employed a local architect, H. E. Goodridge,
to build him yet another folly. Its
combination of 'Picturesque' irregularity
with rigid geometry and archaeological
detail (note the cast-iron turret *à la* Stuart
and Revett's *Antiquities of Athens*) make
Lansdown Tower a key monument in the
development of British Neo-classicism.

These terrible practices, such as using columns, pediments and cornices as decoration, were continued by the Palladian school in England, who made matters worse by popularizing their vices in pattern-books for surveyors and builders – vices such as attached or semi-columns and rustication, which Smirke describes as 'an old and incorrigible imposter'. Again and again he emphasizes the simplicity and functionalism of the Grecian style. 'As the moral character is corrupted by luxury', he writes, 'so is art vitiated by the exuberance of its ornaments. . . . An excess of ornament is . . . the symptom of a vulgar and degenerate taste.' 'Exterior architecture', and here one thinks of the British Museum (plates 25, 26), 'is a grave exhibition of talent and being always in the public eye, it cannot condescend to trifle. When art chooses to frolic in masonry, the effect is not only unnatural, but indecorous.'

Throughout Smirke's treatise he repeatedly emphasizes that Greek revivalism is not merely a matter of imitation but of adapting ancient forms to modern needs. He dismisses archaeological antiquarianism as an irrelevance. He condemns the substitution of Greek for Renaissance decoration as architectural transvestism – 'the parts are Greek, but the general forms and character of the composition remain unchanged. [If] Greek orders are displayed exactly as Italian ones were before . . . there is no real difference between Italianized Roman and Grecianized Italian. . . . In fact, if *composition* be not reformed and purged of its Italian impurities, every new importation of the scraps and rakings of Greek remains only exposes the art to dangers of the most serious nature.' 'Rectangular shapes', he concludes, are 'the component materials of every modern work.'

It was this elimination of superfluous ornament, this concentration upon geometrical forms, this emphasis on the asymmetrical and the disparate, which formed the very basis of the Neo-classical revolution, the framework within which the Greek revival operated. Pugin christened it 'the new Square Style of Mr. Smirke'. Cockerell complained

Plates 23, 24
William Wilkins
Designs for Grange Park, Hampshire, *c* 1804
above
Frontal perspective of entrance façade
with hexastyle Doric portico
Pen and wash 13 × 23in.
right
Plan and elevation of side façade
Pen and wash 12¼ × 17½in.
Literature:
J. M. Crook *Haileybury and the Greek Revival:
the Architecture of William Wilkins, RA.* (1964)

Wilkins transformed a 17th-century mansion
by Samwell into the most remarkable
Neo-classical house in Europe. These
designs, deriving from the Thesion and
Thrasyllus monuments in Athens, show the
house as carried out for the banker Henry
Drummond in 1809. The sarcophagi were not
executed. Later additions by Dance,
Smirke, S. P., C. R. and F. P. Cockerell add
considerably to the interest of this important
building, which is now in danger
of destruction.

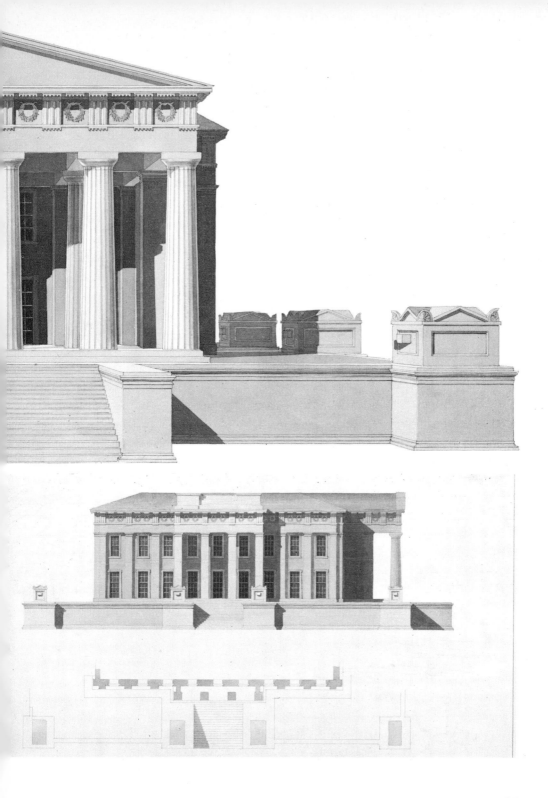

Plates 25, 26
Sir Robert Smirke
Designs for the British Museum, 1836–7
left
North front of the quadrangle
Sepia pen and wash 13¾ × 19in.
below
Principal façade
Lithograph of a drawing by F. Mackenzie
15¾ × 22¼in.
Presented by Mrs. Dorothy Biggar, 1938
Literature:
The History of the King's Works, Vol. V

Smirke designed this Neo-classical landmark
in 1823 but the façade was not complete
until 1847. Even then, the sculptural
decoration shown in the lithograph was never
executed. In 1852–7 the open quadrangle
was eventually filled by the domed
Round Reading Room, designed by
Smirke's younger brother,
Sydney Smirke RA (1798–1877).

Plates 27, 28
William J. Donthorne (1799–1859)
High House, West Acre, Norfolk
Designs for Anthony and Philip Hamond,
about 1823
above
West elevation
Pen and wash 14½ × 20½in.
below
North elevation
Pen and wash 14½ × 25in.

The work was probably executed during
the 1820s, but these elevations may have been
redrawn for publication around 1853.
Donthorne's Gothic designs, such as
Highcliffe Castle, Hampshire (1830–4),
are undistinguished, but his East Anglian
classical schemes like this are examples
of Greek revivalism at its most rigid
and doctrinaire.

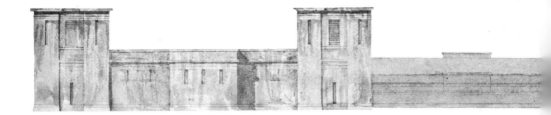

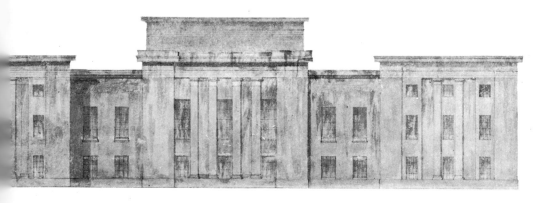

Plate 29
Thomas Hamilton
Project for the Royal High School
on Calton Hill, Edinburgh
Watercolour 30 × 53 in.
In the Royal Scottish Academy, Edinburgh

Literature:
Alistair Rowan, Country Life, 16.11.1967,
p.1254
Three architects in particular helped to
make Calton Hill and its environs into a
'Caledonian Acropolis':

Thomas Hamilton, William Burn and
W. H. Playfair. Hamilton's own Burns
monument is in the centre. In the
background is a view of the old town
with the North bridge, St Giles' cathedral
and the castle rock.

that Wyatt's later exteriors in the Grecian manner, such as Doddington in Gloucestershire, were 'mere blocks of stone'. Such was the opinion of most Victorians. More recently, however, Sir Albert Richardson seized upon the essence of this 'Greco-cubic' style when he remarked that Smirke was 'not content with the mere transcription of Classic orders', but set out to achieve 'original combinations of primary masses'. At Covent Garden Theatre (1809) and in several of his country houses, notably Kinmount (1812), Luton Hoo (1816, much rebuilt), Whittinghame (1818, plate 18) and Normanby Park (1821), Smirke certainly came near to achieving a synthesis of Neo-classical theory and Picturesque composition. Perhaps the most successful examples of this synthesis were erected not in England but in Scotland. They are Hamilton's High School at Edinburgh (plate 30) and 'Greek' Thomson's trio of powerful churches at Queen's Park, St. Vincent's Street and Caledonian Road in Glasgow. The most extreme examples, on the other hand, are all English: Belsay Hall, Northumberland (1810–17), designed by an amateur architect, Sir Charles Monck Middleton, with professional help from Gell and Dobson; Beckford's Lansdown Tower near Bath (1825–6), designed by H. E. Goodridge (plate 22); and an extraordinary composition, High House, West Acre, Norfolk (c 1829) designed by a dim provincial architect, W. J. Donthorne (plates 27, 28).

Predictably enough, the austerities of such a style produced a reaction in favour of purely decorative forms. At one level, this craving for ornament was satisfied by the Gothic revival, moving into its tractarian, ecclesiological or High Church phase during the 1840s. At another level, particularly in secular buildings, the Greek revival gave way to a recrudescence of Renaissance classicism, and here three names stand out: Harvey Lonsdale Elmes, Sir Charles Barry and C. R. Cockerell. In their hands the Grecian style was transformed into a synthetic Renaissance mode which has been variously labelled Greco-Roman, Italianate and neo-Grec. Compare Wilkins's Grange Park (plates 23, 24) with Cockerell's Westminster Life and British Fire Office in the Strand, London (plate 42). Barry's progress from Greek to Italianate is well documented from the Manchester Institution (1824) to the Travellers Club (1829) and Reform Club (1837) in London, and so *via* Bridgewater House (1847) to Shrublands (1849) and Clumber (1857). But the transition from Greek to Greco-Roman is expressed with even greater force in the development of a single building by Elmes: St. George's Hall, Liverpool. Several key drawings in the RIBA collection (plates 35, 36, 37, 38, 40) mark the progress of the overall design. Elmes's original competition designs for the Assize Courts and Concert Hall are conceived in terms which are categorically Greek, yet his fusion of the two buildings in a final design of monumental strength and grandeur shows the architect already moving away from archaeological restrictions (plate 40). The rich polychromy of Cockerell's later interior, modified and completed after Elmes's untimely death, exploits to the full the plasticity and power of Greco-Roman forms (plate 39).

So the heyday of the Greek revival was brief. The popularity of the fashion was more than matched by the violence of the reaction which set in during the 1830s and 1840s. In 1844, Sir Robert Smirke, one-time idol of the Regency, was publicly referred to as 'an architectural Lazarus'. The rise and fall of the movement is a story of slow gestation, explosive popularity and sudden eclipse.Its stages can be neatly documented by means of quotations from contemporary critics.

Horace Walpole's letter to Mary Berry in 1791 recalls the early days of the Greek revival: 'They who are industrious and correct, and wish to forget nothing, should go to Greece, where there is nothing left to be seen, but that ugly pigeon-house, the Temple of the Winds, that fly-cage, Demosthenes' Lanthorn, and one or two fragments of a portico, or a piece of column crushed into a mud wall; and with such a morsel, and many quotations, a true classic antiquary can compose a whole folio, and call it Ionian Antiquities'. (*Letters* XV, 2822, pp.64–5.)

Plate 30
Thomas Hamilton (1784–1858)
Project for the National Gallery of
Scotland at the foot of the Mound,
Edinburgh, 1848 (not executed)
Watercolour 31 × 54in.
In the Royal Scottish Academy, Edinburgh

Literature:
Alistair Rowan, Country Life, 26.10.1967,
p.1054
Plates 29 and 30 illustrate the remarkable
expansion of public and private building
which turned early 19th-century Edinburgh
into the 'Athens of the North'.

Plate 31
Decimus Burton (1800–81)
Arch and screen at Hyde Park Corner, London
Watercolour 24 × 40½in.
Exhibited at the Royal Academy, 1827
Literature:
Sir J. Summerson *Georgian London* (1945);
P. A. Clarke *James and Decimus Burton*
(1949, RIBA Library MS), p.56
Decimus Burton was never a dogmatic Greek
revivalist. His Corinthian/Composite
triumphal arch is really Greco-Roman in
form and feeling. Built in 1828, it was
originally intended as a royal entrance to
Buckingham Palace from the north, as
shown in this drawing. With his Ionic screen
(1825 – Panathenaic frieze by Herring),
Burton's scheme was the last of several
Georgian dreams – notably by Robert Adam,
Jeffry Wyatt and Soane – aiming at a
monumental 'gateway to London'. Burton's
arch was moved to its present site at the
head of Constitution Hill in 1883. Between
1846 and 1885 it formed the pedestal for
M. G. Wyatt's colossal statue of Wellington,
now at Aldershot. Adrian Jones's quadriga
was added in 1912 as a memorial to
Edward VII.

By way of reply, C. A. Busby's *Designs for Villas and Country Houses* (1808) sets out the argument on behalf of the Greek revivalist: 'Till lately the moderns were ignorant of Grecian architecture, properly so called. It was usually included and confounded with the Roman. There is, however, a very striking distinction. About thirty years since, Stuart and Revett published, from actual admeasurements, a complete and accurate elucidation of all the Grecian buildings then remaining in Athens. This work has ultimately produced a considerable effect on the present taste in Architecture; and now, in almost all new buildings, Grecian members and ornaments are so prevalent as to obtrude themselves on the notice of the most superficial observer. The Grecian style possesses many peculiarities which render it particularly well adapted to small and simple buildings. The *boldness* of its parts gives consequence to the most limited edifices, and its elegant ornaments are admirably suited to domestic buildings; but for the sake of irregularity, and the gratification of vanity, they have, in many instances, been so distorted and disfigured by tasteless professors, as scarcely to retain any traces of their beautiful original.'

These latter criticisms of the dilution and distortion of the Grecian style were taken up and expanded, naturally enough, by leading Gothicists. A. W. Pugin was by far the most vitriolic. Writing to Lord Shrewsbury in 1842, he describes Decimus Burton's new town *à la Grecque* at Fleetwood in Lancashire, as follows: Fleetwood 'is the abomination of desolation; a *Modern Greek* town is quite insupportable. I am sitting in a Grecian coffee room in the Grecian Hotel with a Grecian mahogany table close to a Grecian marble chimney piece, surmounted by a Grecian scroll pier glass, and to increase my horror the waiter has brought in breakfast on a Grecian sort of tray with a pat of butter stamped with the infernal Greek scroll. Not a pointed arch within miles. Everything new and everything beastly.'

The violence of this Victorian reaction to the Regency Greek revival is most dramatically represented in Ruskin's diatribe against the style

Plate 32
George Wightwick (1802–72)
Design for a chimneypiece 'adapted from the
Portico of the Temple of Pandrosus'
Pen and coloured wash 16 × 12½in.
Wightwick worked as Sir John Soane's
assistant before moving to Plymouth in
1829, where he inherited the West Country
practice of John Foulston, as well as his
eclectic tastes. Wightwick's sketchbooks
include designs in Gothic and Italianate
as well as Grecian style.

Plate 33
Sir Robert Smirke
Sketches of two Greek vases
Pencil and watercolour $8\frac{3}{4} \times 11\frac{1}{4}$, $9 \times 11\frac{1}{4}$in.
Between 1801 and 1805, Smirke travelled
extensively in France, Italy, Germany and
Greece. These vases were sketched by him at
Girgenti (Agrigento) in Sicily, where their
owner, Don Gaetano M. Sterlini, was
British Consul. Both drawings form part
of a large collection recently discovered
in Somerset.

Plate 34
William Wilkins
London University
(later University College, London)
Engraving from Shepherd & Elmes
Metropolitan Improvements or
London in the Nineteenth Century, 1827–8
Unlike his National Gallery in London,
Wilkins's combination of portico, stepped
stylobate and dome was eminently successful
at University College. Wightwick called it
'next to the dome of St Paul's, the finest piece
of Greco–Italian architecture which I have
ever seen'. It was begun to designs by
Wilkins and Gandy-Deering in 1827.
Wilkins's design for the wings was never
completed. Later additions by
T. L. Donaldson (1848–51), T. H. Lewis
(1869–81) and F. M. Simpson and
A. E. Richardson (1911–24) have all
failed to match up to the original.

in *The Stones of Venice* (1851–3): The Grecian style is 'utterly devoid of all life, virtue, honourableness or power of doing good. It is base, unnatural, unfruitful, unenjoyable, and impious. Pagan in its origin, proud and unholy in its revival, paralysed in its old age . . . an architecture invented . . . to make plagiarists of its architects, slaves of its workmen, and Sybarites of its inhabitants; an architecture in which intellect is idle, invention impossible, but in which all luxury is gratified, and all insolence fortified.'

Another critic, James Elmes, a prolific journalist and the father of Harvey Lonsdale Elmes, explains the anti-Greek reaction of the 1830s and 1840s in more temperate language: 'We had converted Greek architecture into the most humdrum sort of design. Nay it seems to have paralysed our powers of design and composition altogether, so that the only alternative left was to escape from it by plunging *headlong* into the Gothic and Italian styles.'

And so the eclectic reaction was born. The Greek revival received a very bad press from Victorian journalists. As one commentator put it, Grecian buildings 'may be chaste, [but] as the man said of his aunt Deborah, they are so confoundedly prim and ugly that their chastity is proof against all suspicion'. Since then the pendulum of fashion has swung back slowly. It was not until 1914 that Sir Albert Richardson published his *Monumental Classic Architecture*, and not until the 1920s that John Betjeman 'first found Cheltenham sublime'.

Plates 35–40
Harvey Lonsdale Elmes (1814–47)
Assize Courts and St. George's Hall,
Liverpool, Lancashire
These six drawings by a young architectural
genius illustrate the development of what is
generally agreed to be one of Britain's
finest classical buildings. Elmes had won two
complementary competitions in 1839–40
for a new concert hall (plate 38) and for new
Assize Courts (plates 35, 36, 37). Both
designs were then combined (plate 40) and
work began in 1842. Elmes meanwhile
developed tuberculosis and retreated first to
Germany and then to Jamaica, where he died
at the age of 34. The structural work on
St George's Hall was completed by
Robert Rawlinson, 1847–51, and the
gorgeous interior by C. R. Cockerell, 1851–4.

Plate 35
Main façade of the Courts on the site of
1839–40 (not executed)
Pencil and sepia wash 8 × 12½in.

Plate 36
Another design for the façade of the Courts,
1839–40 (not executed)
Pencil and sepia wash 14 × 19¼in.
The tower has a taller lower stage to
increase its height. The podium is
decorated with a sculptured frieze.

Plate 37
Harvey Lonsdale Elmes
Finished competition perspective for the
Assize Courts, Liverpool, Lancashire,
1839–40
Pen and sepia washes 24¼ × 37¾in.
Literature:
C. H. Townsend, RIBA Journal, XIX,
1912, p.445

Plate 38
Harvey Lonsdale Elmes
South façade of St George's Hall, Liverpool,
Lancashire, 1839
Watercolour 23½ × 37½ in.
This competition perspective shows a
corner of the Assize Courts in the
right foreground.

Plate 39
Harvey Lonsdale Elmes
Longitudinal section showing the
interior of St George's Hall, Liverpool,
Lancashire
Pencil, pen and watercolour 14¾ × 25¼in.
Elmes's interior designs were modified
and completed by C. R. Cockerell

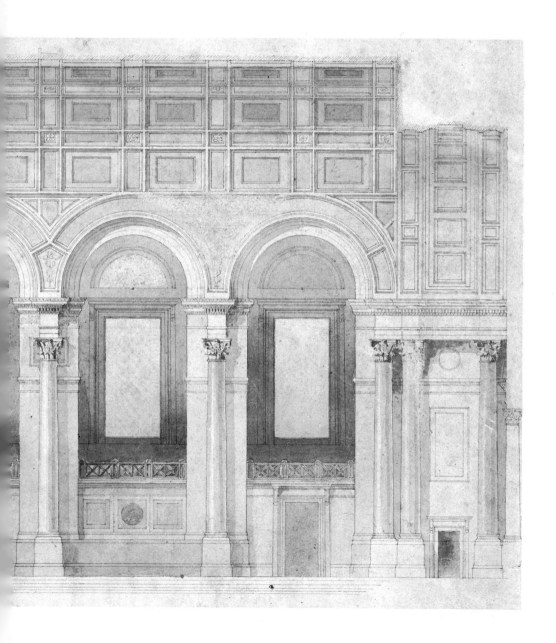

Plate 40
Harvey Lonsdale Elmes
St George's Hall and Assize Courts,
Liverpool, Lancashire, 1840
Pencil and watercolour 16¼ × 20¼in.
Literature:
Walter Millard, RIBA Journal, XVII, 1910,
p.599; Rudolf Dircks, RIBA Journal,
XXVII, 1920, p.88
This sketch shows the revised and final
design, uniting the two buildings in one
structure, from the north east. Alterations
to the apse at the north end are incorporated.

Plate 41
Sir Robert Smirke
The New Post Office,
St Martin le-Grand, London, 1823–9
Engraving from Shepherd & Elmes
*Metropolitan Improvements or London
in the Nineteenth Century*, 1827–8
The New Post Office was built following a
complex and unsatisfactory competition and
cost over £250,000. With the British Museum,
it was London's largest public building in
the Grecian style. The order was that of the
Ionic temple of Athena at Priene in Asia
Minor (illustrated in *Ionian Antiquities*, 1769).
The building was demolished in 1912.

Plate 42 (*left*)
Charles Robert Cockerell
Westminster Life and British Fire Office,
Strand, London
Design for the entrance façade, 1831
Exhibited at the Royal Academy, 1832
Pen, pencil and watercolour 21¼ × 15½in.
Presented by Mrs F. M. Noel
Literature:
J. H. Worthington, RIBA Journal,
XXIX, 1932, p.270; G. M. Young, *ed.*,
Early Victorian England, 1934;
P. Ferriday, *ed.*, *Victorian Architecture*, p.114.
This celebrated building, carried out to a
slightly modified design in 1831–2, was
unfortunately demolished in 1908.

Plate 43 (*below*)
Sir Charles Barry (1795–1860)
Measured drawing of an acroterion from the
Parthenon, Athens, 1818

Pen and sepia wash 8½ × 6¾in.
Barry made only one Grand Tour. He set
out in 1817 and travelled alone through
France and Italy, and then to Greece
and Turkey with Charles Eastlake,
W. Kinnaird (editor of the last volume of
Stuart's *Athens*) and a Mr Johnson. After
going to Egypt, Syria and Palestine, he
returned to England in 1820. Eastlake recalls
for us the excitement and amateurism of
these Regency archaeologists: 'Our luggage
[is] small – mine consists chiefly of materials
for drawing and painting . . . and a mattress
for each . . . ; and we take Pausanias,
Anacharsis, and maps . . . I have no other
object than the picturesque, and shall
consider myself at liberty to put the mosque
and the temple in the same picture, and
to pay the same attention to the Turk's
beard and turban, as to the bas-relief
he sits on'. (*Contributions to the Literature
of the Fine Arts*, 1870, p.72.)

Further reading list

The author is engaged on a full-scale study of British Greek revival architecture, to be published by Country Life. Meanwhile, the best introduction is still Sir Albert Richardson's *Monumental Classic Architecture in Great Britain and Ireland during the 18th and 19th centuries* (1914).

Sir John Summerson
Architecture in Britain, 1530–1837 (1963 edition).
This classic work places the movement in its historical context

Henry-Russell Hitchcock
Architecture: 19th and 20th centuries (1963 edition)
Examines the movement's international significance in magisterial fashion

Emil Kauffman
Architecture in the Age of Reason (1955)
A provocative and idiosyncratic attempt to analyse the theoretical premises of Neo-classicism

Peter Collins
Changing Ideals in Modern Architecture, 1750–1950 (1965)
A challenging study which throws new light on the movement's intellectual origins

H. Levin
The Broken Column (1931)
J. Spencer
Fair Greece, Sad Relic (1954)
W. St Clair
Lord Elgin and the Marbles (1967)
These three books deal with Regency archaeology, tourism and connoisseurship

H. M. Colvin
Dictionary of English Architects, 1660–1840 (1954)
This invaluable work contains biographical studies of all the leading English Greek revivalists

H. Hawley
Neo-Classicism, Style and Motif (1964)
D. Irwin
English Neo-Classical Art (1966)
Explain the parallels between Neo-classical architecture and similar stylistic developments in painting and sculpture

J. M. Crook
Haileybury and the Greek Revival (1964)
J. M. Crook
Architect of the Rectangular: a reassessment of Sir Robert Smirke, Country Life, 13.4.1967
J. M. Crook
Sir Robert Smirke, a centenary florilegium, Architectural Review CXLII (1967), pp.208–10
For summaries of recent research on Wilkins and Smirke

G. Law
'*Greek*' *Thomson*, Architectural Review, CXV (1954), pp.307–16
A. J. Youngson
The Making of Classical Edinburgh (1966)
Alistair Rowan
The Athens of the North Explored, Country Life, 26.10.1967, 16.11.1967
For the Greek revival in Scotland

T. Hamlin
Greek Revival Architecture in America (1944)
For the Greek revival in the United States